I0161873

Houses

Poems
by Homer Starkey

aventine press

Published by Aventine Press
55 East Emerson St.
Chula Vista CA, 92101
www.aventinepress.com

ISBN: 978-1-59330-974-9

Printed in the United States of America

Poems

Impressionist	7
Fear of Speaking, Publicly, to Death	9
Mjolnir	11
Bliss	13
Vapid	15
Penultimate	17
In Those Torched Fields	19
Surfeit	21
It's Just That I	23
Dark Morning	25
What to Do When the World Ends	27
Leaves, Autumn	29
Quantum	31
To a Woman Crossing Gessner Road	33
God Child	35
Egret, R	37
Leap	39
Of California	41
Constellation	43
Middle Eight	45
Isma'il	49
Hoi Polloi	51
Capitol	53
Royalty	55
Carnivore	57
East	59
Inverness	61
Restless	63
Wake	65
That You Call Love	67
We Laughed at the Fat and Happy	69
Halogen Moon	71
Over	73

Yes, Girl, Just a Little Lower   75
We   77
Starship Letter   79
Hayley   81
Birthday   83
A Favor   85
Second Life   87
Ghosts   89
Man-o'-war   91
Transit   93
We've Even Lost   95
Said   97
Sprang   99
Here Ya Say   101
Vision Revision   103
Houses (Without Walls Cannot Exist)   105

for Liam, who has fun with words

Impressionist

I thought you were evil
Turns out
You were just an artist

Fear of Speaking, Publicly, to Death

The words do not flow
When talking to a headstone—
Looking around for eyes
Eyes with ears and lips that speak
Garrulous and prying eyes
Judging my words
As caterwauling
Laughable
Bile

Mjolnir

Born in August
And on a Thursday
Could have been a thunder god
Smash that frost giant with my mighty hammer
And save the world somehow
With a masculine show
Of force
Then
Toss a few dwarfs onto
Balder's pyre

Bliss

She flung herself from Minerva's brow
Springing eternal
Never understanding
Who I am

Hates it when I call her beautiful
Blushes, giggles, uncomfortable
What words to choose
To please the perfect muse?

She—discharged from Athena's gun
Hollow-point princess, drawn by fire
Never knowing
What I show

Loves it when the words come
Gets nervous, then gets her nerve
What has love been
Before this?

She came to me from Minerva's brow
Launched from Athena's bow
She swims in eternal ignorance—
Will she ever win?

Vapid

She
Dissipates
Like vapor trails from an airplane
And I look into the dissolve and see
Visions of my youthful passion
Fade
Into the distant blue

I cannot think of her
Without thinking of the cruel joke
Life has played on me:
Half of one in the hand and
Infinite amounts glaring from the bush

My demise arrives with the thought of possibility
Oh
If this proves to consume me
Then
Dump me into that repository of fools that
Break the souls of women
To satisfy their self-conception

Penultimate

I love you as the sky swallows you whole
    to leave only memory, unreliable newborn

Destinations become cruel promises—
    I wait at the ticket gate

For one dopamine glance to quell
    the desire for you—my soon-forgotten expatriate

I begin again, doomed to sort through baggage,
    trying not to smell you, hear you, mourn the
    complement of you

I loved you, even as the sky swallowed you whole—
    even as I took another penultimate lover

In Those Torched Fields

I collect remnants of you
Pieces unable to fit
Together to form
Arrogance and innocence

I, too, wounded
By harsh experience
That cancers the body
And robs the boy of the smile

I try not to
Roam
In those torched fields of my
Youth

Somewhere I must have expected
You to save me—selfish
As the day I was born
Wanting warmth and nothing else

Surfeit

Wine steals you away,
Beds you down
With its melancholy song

In one ear whispering promises
Just after it asks you to dance
Then turns, and turns
My words into quilled projectiles
Deadly in their accuracy

I am no marksman
Just a fool, no yeoman
But I serve you

I can't chastise
When I dance as well
Thinking all the while
I take the lead—
Devouring those same promises

When will we dance
And turn together
And leave that sure-footed
Disease against the wall?

It's Just That I

Don't visit your grave
        Any longer
Not that I feel
        Any stronger
Or that my mind
        Tends to wander
It's just that I—

Didn't pick up
        The telephone
Not because I
        Wasn't home
Or that I want
        To be alone
It's just that I—

Wasn't at the game
        The boy played
Not wanting to show
        An hour late
Or criticize him
        At the plate
It's just that I—

Didn't pray in
        My foxhole
Not that I think
        I have no soul
Or the spirit has
        No place to go
It's just that I—

Dark Morning

Dark morning is the best
So early, too tired to think about
Lost loves, lost hopes, debt

For a few minutes or more
If you are so inclined
You feel like the last person on earth

And you don't know why this comforts you
You worry that it doesn't concern you
Loves dead, hopes and debt irrelevant

Syphoning gas, eating from cans
Fighting off predators
Is as romantic as it gets

Then that moment you turn on the TV and
A semi-attractive anchor reads the teleprompter to remind you
In thousands of years human nature hasn't really changed

Collective consciousness progresses, regresses
Like a determined heart pumping blood
Steadfast and unaware of its purpose

Dark morning is the best
So early—too tired to contemplate
You're just one push through the vein

What to Do When the World Ends

When cougars lose their claws
When rednecks don't say "y'all"
When porn stars want to cuddle
The remaining sane should huddle

When praised poets fill stadiums
When Texas belles won't wear their mums
When husbands tell wives, "I understand"
We should all come up with a plan

Leaves, Autumn

We fall, are grieved, decay
Like the sins we bring,
Our imperfections,
Our championed things

Now the world of lofty song—
These bucolic gardens—
Fossilize in disrepair;
The heart and phloem hardens

Our punishment is this:
Not limbo or hell or black,
But days finding ways to make more days,
None of which exact

Quantum

I learned of infinite possibilities
Oh, I—I learned of infinite hope
But the other side of infinity
Disturbed me—
The angle of infinite loss

I lost you in infinite ways
Infinite times—at times—
At times by my
Foolish deeds, my strays
And other ways
Other times
I watched
And then wished you away

To a Woman Crossing Gessner Road

Crossing the busy street
With mobile telephone at your ear
You know the speeding cars won't strike you
And, or, even if they do—
What do you have to lose?

A monthly minimum payment
    to Manhattan
A dubious plan for world domination
    (through song)
A void where once you housed
    religion
A host of items, non-biodegradable,
    that
Despite their resistance to nature
    their resistance to adhere
        to her laws,

Will be lost

God Child

The child who built the world—
Who experimented with putty—
Left it frail,
Left it faulty

But upon returning
Gave us clay and sand
And stood beside us
Until we could make shapes

Now

That we've fashioned swords
Knives and guns and
Machines—

That we've stylized our
Own demise—

That we've hardened
The soil that composed
Our late souls—

We've made the child who built the world
See it now—
Frail,
Faulty

Egret, R

We sit upon the boughs
Watching the snipes in flight
If we could
Just
Maybe
We might

Reclaim the what ifs
Gather locals, raise an army
Get back what we took from ourselves
Robust
Zestful
Haughty

We make our way down
Finding a cool dry shade
Tree; beneath it we'll teach and learn—
For us
Maybe
There exists a place

Leap

O,
How did I leap!
How did I leap?
    With the vices
    That slowly creep
    Into a child's soul

O,
When did I sleep?
When will I sleep?
    Creepers in my
    Dreams still crawl—
    Now they've taken hold

Of California

Hey, hey silver screen
From your innocence what might I glean?
Purtiest girl I ever seen
With a pair of eyes
Like the wild tangerines
Of California

Hey, why you smile?
Way out here it ain't fine
Daydreamers die
Daydreamers die
Daydreamers die in Holly
Wood, California

Hey, who you choose?
I invoke thee for my muse
And I'll buy you a new set of shoes
If you can save me
From the tight'nin noose
Of California

Hey, you finally died
And the mandarins are rolling wild
Way down Interstate 5
And Cortez can only smile
Swimming in the Gulf
Of California

Constellation

And the stars
Amorous and blithe
Got jealous
And they ripped you
From the sky
But I still see you
In the absence of light

Middle Eight

I wish my world was one where
Violence was as anomalous as a comet
Where I could trust friendship and passion
And my lover spoke to me

I wish my world was one in which
Past assaults could be reversed
In which my son could not easily recognize
A broken soul

I want our refrain
(Now I speak to you, silent one)
I want it to be
Enviable, taboo
Where we grow accustomed to
Gasps followed with laughter
In the unfocused world
That spins around us

I want him
To know by example
To mimic the memorable
A new chord learned
With his tiny fingers
A new continent discovered
But always misspelled
This hardening of my throat
Is as much for him
The death of possibility
As it is for us

I know our world is, underneath
Full of glory and chance
If only we weave it between our fingers
And claim it again

I hope our world is not
Colliding slowly with a bright star
And we are running toward each other
And regret is the final thing we see

I want a chorus with you
Praising rebirth and parenting
But it's nowhere within any pages
It's nowhere in affirmations
From strangers

We alone know the key
Just we know the progression
The tempo and
The middle eight
That will lead us back
To the familiar, not
The all too familiar

Isma'il

My blood, my son, you seem to reverse time
Growing younger as I grow old, but still
Make youth right here, never there, now yours and mine
Tomorrow you will be too tall, but will

Own those fancies of the heart when life seems
Pale and cold and dry and most desolate
Just know what truth imagination brings
You, the cartographer of your own way

You, engineer of songs they will transcribe
Remember life is not pure existence
But verse the poet wrote free of any rhyme
Make it your own, the world you own, sweet prince

And don't be like the one poor Horatio
Held and whispered a solemn goodnight to

Hoi Polloi

We the many sleep inside a Hollywood bed
We so many subjected to the Hollywood no
Eat the hock end in nearly two squares
Yet always deny hunger while
Dancing the Highland fling
Before short victory

With a hive mind, we high tail
To share the air of higher animals
Those high-colored gods who fell to dirt
Then took our horses
Farthest from the stable door
Leaving we the many pedestrian to walk

Underneath most everything
These hours with heavier hearts
These days with softer desires
Humping, huffing to the distant
Tunnels of our rest
Turning the camera on ourselves

Capitol

Exile—one bedroom
Inside a stew of promised laughs that
I hear sometimes in bed
That big taunting reminder says
"Go ahead and sleep and get older"

"The world exists only as far as you can see
The rest imaginings,
The past imaginings—
Tomorrow totally man's invention"

Still I long, here alone
Embracing my reptilian brain
That served me so well in youth

It's not all laughter three flights down
To the street (Someone once yelled "Kill me!")
But it's alive
  And rich in irony
  And dramatis personae
  And
I in exile can join in
I have money and little ambitions

Royalty

I sit on a second-hand chair
With first-hand knowledge of my sin—
That is, not being in cahoots with Sisyphus—instead
Steadily retreating into that safe base

Seated, on someone's abandoned throne
Playing the jester and the once and fallen king
Simultaneously to my subjects
Their laughs corkscrew into my spleen

What is the puppet to do now but watch the heir
Grow older at double speed
While the grey hairs on my beard
Amass an army to slowly strangle me

Carnivore

Birth mother, feeder of soul
Destroyed the nest
Poached the egg

I am abandoned
With abandon

Mirror wall, scratched
Trying to peel back
Countenance, for revelation

I only testify
When called to surface

Somewhere there is bread
Nurturing honey and milk
From the breast of truth

Time is a carnivore
Circling me

East

Streets of East Downtown
Are cold and quiet at night
Empty of desperation, void
Of identity, calling me

Fences topped with razor
Wire, keeping trapped worth
In, dusty curiosities
At this hour nothing could
Be innocent

Graffiti goes unmolested
Respected—a babe born that
Never ages but grows
Faceless over time

Workers scramble home
Reverse vampires
As the sun sets—brave
Ones stay to change fate

Inverness

As soon as he has tasted war my dear
As soon as the tongue touches blood
He will be of no use to us, I fear
In every
And all accounts of love

We must fix our minds on cheerful
Futures, and shelf irregular madness

We must play the roles God has
Deemed in this damp and dark Inverness

As soon as he hears of truce my dear
As soon as the hand ceases to shake
He will be useless and cold yet near
And the one
We shall all forsake

Restless

Restless boy, outside for you
Almost a punishment, a chore
But it is summer in Houston
I know about summer in Houston

One day can we talk of books and life?
I am as restless as you, it seems
Someday if I am fortunate we will
I want eternal sleep only after I am certain

You will sacrifice for others
But not sacrifice yourself
You will build homes and comfort
You will teach love and strong will

Restless one, my only god
Raised from the remnants of war
Make me forget, make me forget
Years wasted on trivialities

Someday we will talk, or you will talk to me
And teach me things I never could understand
Discarding fear like old stationery
Old words, ignorant thoughts gratefully lost

Restless, restless youth
You give me restful sleep

Wake

Life is not supposed to be
It should not exist
According to the laws of physics

Take the physic
The apothecary said casually
Up to twenty but no more than forty-three

Sentimental fool, I have come
Here to map a journey
As the sentinel conspires against me

Life is not all that
He adds, missing out on an adjective
Retort? I couldn't be bothered to give

And how am I to sleep
I ask before he gives his headshake
Sleep? You came to me to awake

That You Call Love

Once was love, so much, and to death
Till ultimate breath traveled out through the neck

One time more to exhale and to think
That is the test of life, as well, and you blink

But life is long; so long it's a curse
Relax and let biological need take a turn

Cloud your reason with surreal wondrous things
You make sense of—and call love, and call love

Once was love, somewhere soon, and no sleep
Till the indefatigable succumbed to fatigue

Oh, the times we decided what was to be real
Only soil or fire or depths of water will we feel

When life is gone, it won't be long, it won't be worse
Relax and let cosmology and cosmetology laugh in turn

We Laughed at the Fat and Happy

We were kind, forgave and that
Gave us strength to populate the rock
With mounds of farm-raised fish and
Whole-wheat bread for the children
(It's okay to eat fish, Kurt said)

We were tired, but that conducted energy
Straight to the mind—there were
Infinite chances to be taken, and
We laughed at the fat and happy
Who died clutching great wads of cash

We grew old before thirty, seizing
Easy opportunities; the dead died
Solely to teach us we weren't better
Or even that much different, so there!
(Pangaea getting the band back together)

We now quietly despise, lash out
On occasion when we are told, before pulling
A muscle and retreating to our organics,
Our hand-crafted wooden furniture,
The hand-stitched satchels and online wish lists

We were the promise, the faith, the desire
From a virgin universe, representing
Stomped upon ¾-time songs of
What sapiens could attain
Now content, somewhat overweight

Halogen Moon

It was I who called upon you, checked on your
Verticalness, satisfied with long pauses and
Lulls in locution, for I had to be

But this selective amnesia that seems reserved
It rapiers—nay, it promises

You won't remember

You won't remember

My silence, my distant gaze, is not me
Resigning—it's protection of what
I have left

I phoned, unprovoked, to see what was
Still alive in you

You won't remember

I cried and begged and starved myself

You won't remember

For years I bled myself until I could
Not differentiate a halogen light from
The moon overpowering the night

You won't remember

Over

It's been said, although I had to force
It from your breath, stick my arm
Down your throat to pull out the words:

Words no lover wants to learn
Words no mother's son can surmise
Words to make corpses wind from hurt
Words in the end, at the end, no surprise

They've been said, hesitantly then
With conviction and tears of self pity
Once evacuated, talk about the mundane
As nothing happens

Yes, Girl, Just a Little Lower

Let me raise this corpse from death
Like my father did his
Long-sufferer of relationships
Everyone was his last breath

Why would you promote love?
When you know the soul is searching
Always a soul is searching
For hymns and spice and blood

Here am I, speaking from need
Of a warm hand for my shoulder
Of a woman's touch somewhat lower
Of a woman's woman: wounded, free

Let me toast to the festering body
The pathetic *pater familias*
Who said riots and made love like fists
Hitting stained pavement, cracked concrete

For his heart muscle ceased to clench
On that late morning in October
Yes, girl, just a little lower
And I've always seen him since

We

Once told of your aggressions
You became the victim
Sought validation from those who fear you most

But we don't fear you any longer
We see the razors suspended in the honey jar
On that shelf above the dripping faucet

One day you're going to forget and crave sweet
And maybe those rusty things will tear
The demons out from your insides

One day you'll repent and regret
And we will be far from your hands
And your particular words
That make some sense to you

We hope for you and we forgive you and we
Long for others to do so

Too

Starship Letter

When we are 50 years, and 50 years lay ahead
We will maybe probably hopefully eventually
Learn the sick needed care, not that
Dogs needed sweaters, or cats needed love
Or we needed to think more of ourselves

There are species of things, like ferns
That aren't to return

We've found new homes, new inhabitable rocks
Circling stars, circling something
We've done it with fierce purpose
So we can leave our inadequacies
Even for a moment under the engine hum

But our rattling bones will follow us
And we will bang them against the walls

When this century has past
We will happily lay our heads
Victorious on barren sand

Hayley

Lost men, because the wealthy yearn to war
Lost friends: amigos, comrades—today, tomorrow's yore

Not a single reality, just daydreams between concussions
Between supper and sex and song and screams
Not a care in the nebula for you, because you—
Apologies in advance—aren't close to becoming these

Lost then, a girl who rights the course
Writing a post, praising the lonely
Lost ends, hopefully dead—death the consummate teacher
The essence and compassion and understanding

Some don't notice

Birthday

There is a bond, black
As the morning you were born
A flipped pickup truck
Transporting no tools
(Only empty beer cans
And unfiltered cigarettes)

A happy girl, life wide open
Eyes brilliant green
The color of well-fed lawns
Died long before she offered you

But the blood ran its course
And air entered your lungs
And you cried for the first of many times
Rejecting life and its series of passages

There is a bond, black
As the deep mirror that exposes you
That man never died
When the Chevy rolled twice
To crush his skull
He sees you even now

The girl is still looking, looking
Looking through green-grass irises
And she is hoping
Hoping

A Favor

We make our way down to the pit of vipers
To save the newborn foal, fallen
Silent, we don't know if it shakes
From the newness of life
Or fright

Before risking
Lethal injection by way of natural selection
Thought strikes head, and we realize
Why our first breath
Is a wail
Why the terminally ill are
At peace
Why there is no alien life
Cold calling Earth

And we climb back up

Second Life

In the next world I suspect
You will torment me
Remind me of my faults
Even when, then, as now, they will be
Inconsequential.

On the next plane of life and love
You will beseech me
Tell me stories, long anecdotes
Of those in your sight and mind
That run long perfect circles around me.

No matter what death, you murder me.
Even after death, I long to die again.

Ghosts

Don't
Read into these words;
Just words
Words

You
Never speak to me,
Just punch
Letters

Don't
Think too much of this
When now it's
Easy

And
Do not ask me to
Be a shell—
I won't

Don't
Read into these words;
Just listen,
Listen,

Listen
To a heart's cry for blood
And two
Lungs enabling

Four
People in this room:
Two ghosts
And their hosts

Man-o'-war

It's your mind
That's torn a world apart
It's my mind
That brings fin back to start
Of the mind
That the chemicals compete for you
Of the mind
That by now
I should know
What's

To be done
As I seal the cracked window
What's to be donned
As your soul it comes it goes
And I'm done
Blaming gravity for the fall
Not really done
Blaming myself for all

It's my mind
That keeps mining memories
It's your mind
That seldom sees the sea I grieve
And highest tides
Sand and words scrawled 'tween the weed
Those never words
Just fingertips and nails
Scratching man-o'-war stings

Transit

Take the train
To
Everywhere—

I
Will meet you
There.

We've Even Lost

We've even lost
And all night
We'll want false lies
To walk away with something

But loss will not justify
The things that we are to do,
Romantic and hopeless

Even if the smaller things
That we collect
Could help create a bridge
To cross some chasm

Nothing would sort beneath, the
Clean and corrupt and cruel

What we cannot give
We will not give, you
Should not expect us
To give

Said

Said we those descriptions
That needed to be said
Now need to die—
Now need to be

The best versions of themselves
Long, long after
Fires consume forests, which
Rise again tree by tree

To block that blinding dusk
Borne of arrogance
To bulwark that blinding dust
Of self-imagining

That impetuous tryst
Unseen by youth
A pre-packaged identity
Justified by word of mouth

Sprang

Run toward the voice familiar
Let feet crunch them
Broken bones

Splayed out to impede
Such horrible future
But that sound, that sound—

It knows

Here Ya Say

You bruit, brute—
Here ya say, hirsute—
And warm in the cold of the ice that came
From tears from the eyes of the degenerate hopeful

I calm, come—
There's a hotspur, son—
Told to be bold in the face of the nameless
Horde and become bored of the lovely vainglorious

Atoll, stranded
Wind carries voices
Only so much to punish us

You perfect, specimen—
Lab pig, decadent—
Leader of the rodents and the snakes who would
Swallow them whole to gain respect as they should

I bleed, out—
Tested positive, negative—
Ensconced in velvet and pine and dead soil
Grow a bush then a tree then rage the topmost

Concrete, over us
We don't scream at all
Can't breathe, even breathe, never

Vision Revision

At the table—
Here sits the lovers scorned
The sanctimonious crowding
For the head, to be first served
Some type of retribution
Oh, they would have my skull
Oh, they would wrap my soul
In a wet blanket
And leave it out for the sleet and rain

Vision:
The boy leading his ox, head shaved
Wearing maroon and gold
Smiles at me—he knows I must die
And try again to become Buddha

After we dine—
Supped on memories of my wrongdoing
As if I were the sole party in sin
They slice with eyes my thinning skin
They keep blades at bay until it opportune
And how I miss that lengthy discomfort
Just minutes ago at the table
Where I pulled up a stool, they pulled out a bench
And made me sit naked

Revision:
That boy did smile
But at someone behind me

Houses (Without Walls Cannot Exist)

Mirror:
I might see all causes
Blocked ambitions, healing sores
Trauma revisited, hardly dismissed
DNA pulling me toward familiar pain

There's quiet outside save the crunch of fresh snow
Accompanied by a solitary huff
Mind gets accustomed to cold
To the thought of heart's final thoughts

Bright light from a sky that never shows
A true face, only colors mixed with promised rains
You somehow smell from your cell and touch walls
Layered in flesh, the skin of someone

The only one that speaks, half-blinded wretch
He's murdered more than one could even count
Or want to—but an only friend, confidant
Never forgets the date of your birth or your death

Mirror:
I know you are just glass
Slow-moving sand mimicking water
So what should I pretend to be, this last day
Before he speaks of the god who forsakes me?

Special thanks to:

Steve, for the cover design of this collection and being patient with my requests. Ricardo, for the author photograph (although you probably don't remember taking it). Betty, for the notebook that has drafts of these poems, a gift from years ago. And Liam, for inspiring me to be better.

www.ingramcontent.com/pod-product-compliance
Lightning Source LLC
Chambersburg PA
CBHW060121050426
42448CB00010B/1976